WORRIES AN

How to help your ch
and confident

WORRIES AND FEARS

Help your child overcome worries and develop confidence

Dr John Pearce

THORSONS PUBLISHING GROUP

First published in 1989

British Library Cataloguing in Publication Data

Pearce, John 1940 - Oct. 27-
Worries and fears : help your child overcome worries
and develop confidence.
1. Children. Development. Role of interpersonal
relationships with parents
I. Title II. Series
155.4

ISBN 0 7225 1893 5

Illustrations by *Willow*

To Mary

*Published by Thorsons Publishers Limited, Wellingborough,
Northamptonshire NN8 2RQ, England*

Printed in Great Britain by Cox & Wyman, Reading, Berkshire.

1   3   5   7   9   10   8   6   4   2

CONTENTS

INTRODUCTION

Anxiety is the emotion that we experience most frequently —except, perhaps, happiness. But without worries or fear we would be unable to avoid the potentially harmful things that we meet in everyday life. For example, it would be very dangerous to cross a busy main road without being at least a bit worried about the traffic. Anxiety is therefore a necessary and healthy emotion that we all need to protect ourselves. Our children have to be taught to be concerned about and even fearful of the everyday dangers of fire, water, electricity, traffic and so on. However, anxiety is so important for keeping us safe from danger that children are born with an inbuilt fear response to sudden loud noises, heights, and anything unfamiliar or unusual.

Anxiety is infectious and can easily be caught from other people—rather like a virus. This makes worries and fears particularly difficult to deal with because they can pass so easily from the parent to the child or from the child to the parent. Children seem to have a special ability to sense any worried feelings that their parents might have. Even if you try to hide your worries, your child will almost certainly know that something is wrong and that all is not well. In one way, the passing of anxiety from parent to child is important because this is how children learn what to be fearful of, so that they can be protected from harm.

Like so many aspects of bringing up children, a balance has to be struck between not being concerned enough about a child's safety on the one hand, and being over-anxious on the other. Over-protective parents are more likely to have anxious, sensitive children, partly because the parent's worries are easily caught and partly due to lack of opportunity to find out about and learn how to cope with the feared situation.

You may think that I take a rather firm line that could cause children to become upset, but if you read the book carefully you will find there is always a good reason for being tough. You must remember that being loving and being indulgent are not the same thing. Indeed, more trouble is caused by parents giving in 'for a quiet life' than for any other reason. It is not at all easy to stick to what you have said, especially if you are not sure that you are doing the right thing in the first place. However, anxious children gain a great deal of security and comfort from their parents being firm and consistent in the care that they give.

I would like you to feel that I am talking directly to you as you read through the book. You can 'talk' back to me if you don't agree with what I am saying. Then read on and it should become clear why I have taken a certain line rather than any other. Don't hold back from having an argument with me in your head or asking someone else what they think. In this way you will become much clearer about what you believe yourself.

Child care is not so much about right and wrong, but more about finding the best compromise between the various demands of family life. For this reason it is impossible to 'get it right' all the time and, as a parent, this often leads to feelings of guilt. In fact, part of being a parent is feeling guilty about not doing the right thing for your child!

If you are unsure about your own ideas, but have some reservations about what I have written, I would like you to follow my suggestions as closely as possible, in spite of any reservations you might have. I have been very careful to give guidelines and advice only where I am confident that it is safe, reasonable and effective. If you have followed the guidelines and they have not worked, please don't immediately think that I have got it all wrong. It is more likely that you are not sticking closely enough to what I have said. So, read it again, have another go. . . and don't give up!

It is the love you have for your child that makes being a parent so fulfilling and full of joy. But it is the same bond of affection that makes it so painful and distressing when things don't go right. Our feelings of love vary from time to time and fortunately it is not necessary to love your child all the time in order to be a reasonable parent. However, children do need to be cared for and protected from harm. This may mean that you will have to be very firm and decisive and be prepared for your child to be upset and angry because of not getting his or her own way. You may also have to allow your child to experience worries and fear and to face up to anxiety so that they can be mastered and controlled in a constructive and creative way.

At the end of the book there is a section outlining some of the research on anxiety for those of you who would like to have more detail and to read further on the subject. I hope that there is something to interest everyone, even if you have no children. You might even find out something about yourself and the reasons for your own anxiety. After all, we all experience worries and fears!

CHAPTER 1

THE DEVELOPMENT OF WORRIES AND FEARS

Babies spend a lot of time crying, much to the distress of their parents. It is easy to misinterpret the significance of a baby's crying and to imagine that there is more meaning to the crying than is the case. It is easy to think that once you have excluded every obvious cause for your baby crying, that it must be due to some form of distress, probably caused by worry and fear. However, the most frequent cause for babies crying is physical discomfort, such as hunger, indigestion, having a wet or dirty nappy and so on.

Some babies cry just because they are bored and nobody is doing anything exciting with them. Babies do of course cry if they are startled by a loud bang or a sharp pain, but this is not due to any specific emotional state of anxiety or fear—the 'startle response' is more closely linked to an automatic reflex action. It is not until around the age of 6 months that you can be absolutely sure that a baby has an obvious and specific emotional state, where everyone would agree exactly what emotion is being shown by the child. You might think that babies show anger by the way that they scream and go rigid at a much earlier age than 6 months, but this behaviour is very common and most people would find it difficult to be quite sure exactly what emotion was being expressed. It could be anger but it could also be extreme fear, misery or pain. However, when a 6-month-old child shows separation anxiety there is no doubt about exactly what emotion is being experienced.

Separation anxiety

The obvious fear that occurs when a child is taken away from a parent is called separation anxiety. It is interesting to note that the word 'anxious' comes from the Latin word *anxius*, which means to hold tight, and is closely related to the word for anger. The Romans seem to have clearly understood the feelings of separation and also the close relationship between anger and anxiety.

SOME BABIES CRY JUST BECAUSE THEY ARE **BORED**....

The forming of a relationship between parent and young child is called *bonding*. It is a two-way process and happens gradually over a period of years. The bonding of a parent to their child starts before birth, but is at its strongest shortly after birth. On the other hand, the bonding of the child to the parent does not become significant until 5–7 months of age, and then reaches a peak at about a year old. Once this stage is reached, babies can no longer be passed from one stranger to another with ease; they will cry and reach out and cling to their parents. The child-parent bond continues to be strengthened over the next few years. Because bonding is a gradual process, there is time over several years to work on the relationship between the child and parent in order to get it right.

If, during the first five to seven years of life, a child is cared for by someone who is not the parent, for example a foster parent, the child will then become bonded to that person. Children cared for in this way will come to feel that this person is in fact their natural parent, even though they know that this is not the case. Only frequent and close involvement with the parent during this period could stop this from happening. Bonding is therefore a powerful process which must be recognized and understood.

Separation anxiety is a universal feature of all children in any culture. It is worse if the separation occurs in unfamiliar surroundings and if the parent leaves the child rather than the other way round. After the age of 3 years, separation generally causes less distress. However, prolonged separation leads to a recognizable sequence of emotional behaviour, as follows:

1. **protest**—crying, screaming, searching for the absent parent
2. **withdrawal**—detached and quiet, with rather flat emotions
3. **despair**—miserable and listless.

Following a period of separation, young children also show a characteristic behaviour pattern of anger, avoid-

SEPARATION ANXIETY CAN BE RECOGNIZED BY THE FACT THAT THE **STRENGTH** OF THE EMOTION IS AT ITS **MAXIMUM** AT THE POINT OF SEPARATION ....

ance and approach and this may occur in any sequence. This anger and avoidance has spoilt many happy reunions and has been the cause of great confusion for parents, unless they are aware just how normal this is.

Separation anxiety can occasionally become a problem for older children when they start at the nursery or at school or have to go anywhere that is new to them. It can be recognized by the fact that the strength of the emotion is at its maximum at the point of separation and then improves after the separation has been achieved.

Stranger anxiety

By the age of 6 months, most children are starting to show obvious fearful emotions that are much more specific than in younger children. For the first time it is possible to be absolutely sure that a child is anxious, rather than having to guess or work it out by eliminating other causes. Specific fear reactions can be seen in response to heights, strange objects, separations, and strangers. Stranger anxiety becomes very obvious when you realize that you can no longer pass your baby around your friends even to hold for just a short while. Provided a 2-month-old child is held in a comfortable way, you can hand the child to a friend with no crying or clinging, but do the same with an 8-month-old and it would be unusual if the baby didn't protest fairly soon after being handed over.

By 2 years old the child is usually less fearful of adult strangers, but still anxious with other children. At 3 years old, fear of strangers is normally decreasing and it is at this time that you should start to teach your child the important safety lesson that not all strangers are nice. Some children continue to be shy and socially anxious, but, for those who are not, some reawakening of stranger anxiety is helpful.

Parents have to make their children sufficiently careful and suspicious of other adults to be safe, but without terrifying them. It is a task that everybody finds difficult;

however, don't leave it for the school or police to do. The basic training needs to come from you and then to be backed up by what other people say.

It is a good idea to have a set of rules that children can learn as they grow older, and then more freedom outside the home is only allowed when they are reliable in remembering and keeping to the rules. For example:

- learn what a stranger is: a stranger is a man or a lady who has not been inside your home and whose home you have not been inside (get your child to give you some examples so that you can check that the point is understood)
- never talk to strangers you meet in the street or the park even if they seem very kind
- never go anywhere with strangers, whatever the reason they give, even if they ask for help
- never accept anything from a stranger, even if you would like it very much
- learn what to say and do if a stranger does talk to you: 'I have to go home now', and quickly walk or run home (get your child to show you how this would be done)
- learn what to do if a stranger touches you: scream, and shout 'DON'T TOUCH ME!' (get your child to show you how this would be done).

There are a few exceptions to these rules; for example, a doctor or a dentist is a stranger but has to talk to children and touch them. But don't teach your child about any of the exceptions until you are sure that the rules are firmly established.

Childhood fears

Every child will experience a wide range of fears at different stages of development. The following list gives some idea of the most common fears and when they usually occur:

- strangers   6 months–3 years
- animals   2–4 years
- darkness
- storms   } 4–6 years
- imaginary monsters
- mysterious happenings   6–12 years
- social embarrassment
- academic failure   } 12–18 years
- death and wars

On the whole, fears are more common in girls than boys, especially as children grow older. There are probably several different reasons for this, but an important one is that we encourage boys not to show their feelings of anxiety and fear. However, the most significant reason for differences in the way children show fear is their temperament. On the whole, childhood fears are a passing phase,

CHILDHOOD FEAR MAY BECOME A PROBLEM WHEN THE PARENT HAS SIMILAR FEARS....

but they may continue and become a problem in the following circumstances:

- the child has a sensitive, anxious temperament
- the parent has similar fears

- the child has had to cope with other stressful events
- following a bad experience with the fear in real life
- where nothing has been done to help the child over-come the fear
- where the fear has been taken too seriously
- where the fear has been avoided.

If a fear is allowed to continue, it could develop into a terrifying, overwhelming fear; in other words, a phobia. This is most likely to occur in generally anxious children where the fear has been avoided or the child hasn't had the experience of staying with the fear and mastering it.

Night-time fears

Many fears are worse at night. In addition to the fear of darkness itself, it is easy to imagine all kinds of monsters and creatures from outer space lurking in the shadows. This type of fear is most common between the ages of 3 and 7 years, but there is more to this than meets the eye. Many children find that complaining about monsters and burglars in the bedroom is an effective way of delaying bedtime and keeping the parent in the room. It can be very difficult to know just how real the anxiety is, because after a while children come to believe in their own creative imaginings—often with the help of their parents!

Many parents will go to great lengths to prove that an imaginary fear is unreal. For example, checking in the wardrobe to show that there is no burglar there or looking under the bed just to demonstrate that there isn't a monster hiding away. Unfortunately this gives children the message that there is a possibility that they could be there—otherwise why would you be looking? In the same way, keeping a night light on gives the wrong message. A light in the room at night is not necessarily reassuring because it gives children the message that dark is danger-ous. So parents' actions to reassure their children can actually make them more anxious.

Disturbed sleep is very frequent in children. It is the rule for small babies to wake repeatedly during the night and, even at 5 years old, about 25 per cent of children sleep poorly. It is easy to think that night-time fears are the most frequent cause of unsettled sleep, but this is not the case. The lack of a well-established sleep habit is much more common. Many parents actually maintain the poor sleep pattern by always responding to their child's crying, even though there is nothing wrong with the child except for an apparent fearfulness. Children quickly learn how to manipulate their parents into the bedroom, but by going in to reassure, the parents give the wrong message: 'Yes, there is something to be frightened of and I need to come and protect you'. So any imaginary fears that the child might have will become even more real and frightening.

Nightmares are often seen as a sign of anxiety in the child. In most cases this is not so—only a few children with nightmares are also anxious or under stress during the day. Nightmares occur most frequently in the 5–15 years age group and affect about 5–10 per cent of children at any one time, although almost all children will experience them at some time.

Nightmares mostly occur during the rapid eye movement (REM) phase of sleeping. The REM stage of sleep occurs about seven times a night in children, but less frequently in adults. It consists of an increase in, and an irregularity of, breathing, heartbeat, blood pressure and body movement. This is accompanied by rapid movements of the eyes and dreaming.

Nightmares occur most frequently in the latter half of the night and often involve quite a complicated story with frightening events. Night terrors are different from nightmares in the following ways:

● **they occur more frequently in the early part of the night with a sudden arousal from the deepest stage of sleep**

- sleepwalking occurs in a similar stage of sleep
- the child appears to be awake, but is confused, disorientated and may seem to be hallucinating
- the images are terrifying, but simple, with no story attached to them
- in the morning the child will have no memory of the night terror.

Both nightmares and night terrors are more frequent in children than adults and therefore can be seen as part of normal development. These anxiety dreams are not a sign that your child is disturbed or ill in any way, so it is important to encourage the child back to sleep and not to make too much of them (see page 75).

Childhood phobias

A phobia is an overwhelming fear that is irrational and focused on a specific object, such as an insect or bird, or a situation, such as heights or being at school. The strength of the fear is very powerful indeed, to the point where the child is unable to control it and where the fear is quite out of proportion to the way in which most children would normally react. However, in comparison with adults, children's phobias are much more variable, unpredictable and short-lived. Animal phobias and other specific fears are common between 2 and 6 years of age, affecting at least 30 per cent of children in this age group. There is a peak incidence at about 3 years old, but by the start of secondary school almost all children will have grown out of any phobias they might have had.

It is unclear exactly how phobias occur in the first place. There is an obvious developmental aspect which possibly suggests that the combination of an immature nervous system and limited understanding makes a child vulnerable to phobias. In addition it can be shown that many phobias result from a real event involving real fear, for example, being bitten by a dog, or experiencing fear for some other reason when looking at a spider, followed by the spider and the fear becoming linked into a phobia.

Phobias have the following characteristics that distinguish them from worries and anxieties:

- there is no evidence of distress unless the phobic child is near to the feared object
- the fear that is aroused by a phobia is overwhelming and can be paralysing in its strength
- the nearer a child is to the feared object, the worse the fear is, but with anxiety the fear often gets less as soon as the child is faced with the feared situation
- talking about phobias may make them worse, but talking about worries usually makes them better
- phobias have an irrational, inappropriate and often bizarre aspect to them while most anxieties are very understandable.

If a phobia continues into adolescence, it is much more likely to remain into adult life—almost all adults with phobias can trace them back to early childhood. There are well-established ways of dealing with phobias and obviously it is best to catch them at an early stage before they become fixed (see page 78). The main problem with helping phobic children is that they will usually do all they can to avoid the feared object and so they may never find out that there is nothing to be afraid of.

Rituals and obsessions

A ritual is a repeated action that has a special meaning for the person carrying it out. Rituals bring a sense of comfort and a reduction of tension—a bit like scratching an itch! Many, if not all, children develop rituals and this is most often seen between the ages of 5 and 10 years. Here are some examples of rituals:

- repeatedly putting toys, dolls or bricks in a row
- saying the same words or phrases again and again
- making sure that everything in the room is in exactly the same place
- avoiding walking on the cracks between pavements
- doing things one after the other, in exactly the same order
- insisting that other people do things in a particular way
- always doing things in the same way—sitting, eating, dressing, washing
- checking things over and over again
- having to touch objects repeatedly
- feeling an urge to repeat actions frequently.

SOMETIMES THE RITUALS CAN GET **OUT OF HAND** AND **TAKE OVER** THE FAMILY....

Rituals are often used as a way of reducing anxiety. By keeping things the same and familiar, the child is able to feel more at ease and less anxious. Sometimes the rituals can get out of hand and take over the child and even the family as well. If your child has ritualistic behaviour, you should ask yourself the following questions:

1. Is it unreasonable for a child to behave in this way?
2. Is the behaviour interfering with the everyday life of the child or the family?

If the answer to both questions is yes then it is worth while taking action to stop the ritual (see page 49). No harm will come to your child if the rituals are prevented in a firm but kind way. However, you should deal with any underlying anxiety at the same time.

An obsession is similar to a ritual in that it is repeated, but unlike a ritual, an obsession is also resisted and unwanted and involves thoughts more than actions. There is a very close link between phobias and obsessions. In fact, a phobia could be described as an obsessional fear. For example, a dog phobia could be described as an obsessional avoidance of dogs; obsessional hand-washing could be described as a dirt phobia. It is interesting to note that as phobias tend to fade away before puberty, so obsessions increase in frequency. One of the most common examples of an obsession is having a tune 'on the brain'. However, obsessions that interfere with everyday life are rare in children and, if they do occur, they can be dealt with in much the same way as rituals.

Emotions don't obey the rules of physics

Although emotions have a physical basis, they do not obey the rules of physics. There is a common belief that once a person has developed a particular amount of worry, the same quantity has to come out somehow or it will be impossible to stop being anxious. This mistaken idea has led to children (and adults) being encouraged to express their anxiety so that they can 'get it out of their system'. In children this may lead to the development of even more worries and fears. For example, the more you talk to children about the hairy green monster they think lives

THE MORE YOU TALK ABOUT THE **HAIRY GREEN MONSTER** THEY THINK LIVES ROUND THE CORNER, **THE MORE REAL WILL THE FEAR BECOME....**

round the corner and the more they tell you about its details, the more real will the fear become.

Emotions behave in an almost magical way. A large amount of anxiety can sometimes be made to disappear into nothing by developing confidence. On the other hand a small amount of anxiety and fear can remain hidden for years and then quite unexpectedly grow and grow until it gets right out of control. This strange and unpredictable behaviour of emotions is even more noticeable in young children since they tend to have rather uncontrolled and 'pure' emotions.

Which emotion is which?

It has been claimed that mothers can distinguish different types of crying in their baby, and that there are different sound patterns of crying, each with a separate meaning. For example, there might be separate distinctive cries for sadness, pain, anger, boredom, frustration, hunger, discomfort and so on. But most parents have great difficulty knowing what their baby is getting upset about and have to work it out for themselves—you have to be a bit of a detective and ask yourself questions like:

- how long is it since the last meal?
- what else has been happening to the baby recently?
- is the nappy dirty or uncomfortable?
- is the stomach bulging with wind?
- could the baby be lying on a toy or something sharp?
- does the baby seem too hot or too cold?
- is the child ill?

Parents mostly use inspired guesswork. More often than not they get it right, but in the middle of the night this is not always so easy! A frequent mistake that parents make is to assume that when a baby cries it must have the same meaning as when an adult cries. The parent then becomes upset on the child's behalf. However, a baby's crying may be of no more significance than that it is bored and wants to be picked up. On the other hand it could be in agony with terrible 'wind', or be lying on an open safety-pin. Parents come to know the difference between normal crying and desparate crying, but even then it is not always possible to get it right and it may well be that, rather than the baby's cries being very different and specific for each emotion, they just get louder and more desperate the more stressful the situation is.

One way of telling the difference between the various emotions is to look at the expression on the face of the child. Distinct changes in facial expression are noticed from birth onwards, but in the first few weeks the expression is either one of crying or no particular emotion.

THIS OCCASIONAL **SMILING EXPRESSION** DOES NOT APPEAR TO BE RELATED TO ANY **MEANINGFUL EMOTION....**

The occasional smiling expression which is seen at this time does not appear to be related to any meaningful emotion until the age of about 6 weeks. Gradually, as the child grows older, the facial expressions of moods become increasingly more clearly defined and easy for all to recognize.

Children and adults also make typical sounds and gestures associated with different emotions, such as soft cooing sounds when contented and moaning sounds when unhappy. But these are not always well-defined in young children and can easily be misinterpreted. For example, a loud shout may mean pain or pleasure; 'hysterical' laughter can occur with distress or with joy; a smile can be due to anxiety or enjoyment.

Even in adults, it can sometimes be very difficult to know exactly which emotion is which, because adults can train themselves not to show the facial expressions of emotion. In addition, both the physical and psychological symptoms are, to a large extent, shared by all feeling states. The symptoms indicate that something is wrong and that the person is distressed. This may be due to physical or emotional stress or, as is usually the case, both of these together. In fact, it is hard to think of any physical stress which does not have an emotional component to it. For example, hunger pains are certainly physical, but they are often brought on just by thinking about food, or being worried that there may be no food available.

In order to identify which emotion your child is experiencing, you will have to know him or her very well and be able to work out how your child is likely to see the situation in which the emotion is experienced. Nevertheless, it is always easy to misinterpret children's emotional state, particularly when they are very young. This misinterpret-

MOST EMOTIONS ARE MIXED....

ation occurs when a child clings to its mother and she assumes that her child is frightened and anxious about being without her. In fact it is usually the actual process of separation itself that the child finds difficult, rather than being away from the parent afterwards, so as soon as the separation has occurred most children settle down happily —so long as their attention is taken by something of interest.

Most emotions are mixed. For example, jealousy is a mixture of anxiety, anger, and sadness. So it may be difficult to work out exactly what mood your child is in and in many ways it is more important to know that your child is experiencing stress and is emotionally upset than to know precisely what emotion it is.

The link between anxiety and other emotions

Of all emotions, it is anxiety which is the most commonly experienced. It is even more common than anger. There is a very close connection between anxiety, anger and depression, but the nature of the relationship is a complicated one. An emotional reaction occurs as a response to a stress, which may be caused by an event outside a child, such as being told, 'I don't like you', or by an event inside the child, such as the thought; 'I think my parents love my sister more than me'.

Whenever a stressful event occurs, the first feeling to be experienced is anxiety, which explains why it is the most frequently occurring emotion. If the stress is mild then there is unlikely to be any progression to other emotions, but, if the stress increases, sooner or later anger will develop. An example of this would be a boy who is jealous of his sister and is under stress in situations where he could be treated unfairly. When he sees his mother get a bag of sweets out, he becomes anxious that he won't have his fair share and watches carefully, anxiously counting out the sweets. If the sister is indeed given more sweets than her brother, his stress becomes greater and he may then become angry and aggressive. So where there is anger you should always expect to find anxiety as well. You will see this in yourself when you are angry—for example the anxious feeling, the shaking and the 'butterflies in the stomach' feeling.

If the stress continues to increase, the anger and anxiety will also increase until eventually a state of depression and misery may result. You will see this process in the way a temper will often end in tears and unhappiness and, in our example of the jealous boy, he may finally become withdrawn and feel miserable and unloved if he is continually made to feel jealous and angry. Once again, the physical symptoms of anxiety and anger are also the same for depression and misery and you should always expect depression to be accompanied by both anger and anxiety.

Conclusion

The emotions of anxiety and fear are undifferentiated at birth and it isn't until 6 months old that specific fears of separation and strangers can be seen. Different fears appear at different ages and are more transient and variable than in adults. In the vast majority of children, phobias, fears and rituals fade away as adolescence approaches.

CHAPTER 2

HOW TO COPE WITH WORRIES AND FEARS

Children only gradually become aware of worries over the first two or three years of life and they have to depend a great deal on their parents for help and protection. But if parents are over-protective, their children will never learn how to be confident and to cope alone. If, on the other hand, parents don't help and support their children enough, there is a real danger that their children will also find it difficult to cope with anxiety, because they haven't been taught how to manage and control their feelings of worries and fear.

Watch out for your own anxiety

Perhaps the most important thing that anyone can do to help a child who is worried is to be calm and confident in themselves. Anxiety is so quickly passed on from one person to another that being calm may not be all that easy, especially if you are rather anxious by nature. Because children are so close to their parents, it may be very difficult for you to cover up feelings of anxiety and hide them from your son or daughter.

What can you do about this infectious nature that worries have? Some people think that a parent's worries can even be passed on to a baby before birth, so you can't start soon enough. Here are some ideas:

- if you are finding it difficult to be confident and calm, try something easier first
- try to avoid giving up and letting someone else take over from you—this won't give you a chance to get better at dealing with your anxious feelings
- ask other people to give you encouragement
- make sure that you don't let anyone undermine your efforts
- if, in spite of all your efforts, your child has picked up your anxiety, worrying about it won't help—at least you know this is normal and the main thing to watch out for is that you don't get stuck in a circle of anxious concern where each worries about the other worrying!
- don't worry if you find it difficult to be calm and confident—we all do, but some people are better at putting on an act than others; all that is needed is a bit more practice, so don't give up!

Don't be surprised if you feel anxious for your child right from the beginning, especially if he or she is the first born. This is normal and predictable, but in spite of these feelings, try to create an atmosphere of peace and calm at home and be firm and confident in your handling of your child.

Is crying a sign of anxiety?

Children's emotions develop slowly, stage by stage, and it is a mistake to think of a young child as just a small adult. This might lead you to think that if the crying continues after you have done everything you could to make the child comfortable, then it must be deliberately done to annoy you. Parents must watch out for this mistaken idea so that they can avoid being angry and blaming the child without justification.

Remember that toddlers cry easily and it doesn't have the same meaning as when an adult cries. The crying serves as a powerful signal to alert parents to the needs of their baby. However, as the child grows older, there comes a time when it is more helpful for you *not* to respond to every cry, otherwise your child will soon discover that you can be easily controlled, just by crying and being demanding. If children have the feeling that they are in control of their parents, they soon become anxious and insecure. Each parent has to decide when is the right time to become less responsive to their child's crying, but it is best done very gradually and gently, starting from birth and being prepared to be quite firm when necessary from 6 months onwards.

Provided that children's basic needs have been met and they are not ill or in pain, no harm will come from crying, even if it goes on for a very long time. Sometimes parents worry that crying— even if it is just for attention—may do some physical or psychological damage to children and eventually make them very anxious. Fortunately young children are remarkably resilient and they come to no harm through crying, even if it goes on to the point of making themselves sick. However, it is only possible to take this rather tough approach if it is done in the context of loving family relationships and the reasons for *not* responding to the crying have been carefully thought through.

There are very good reasons for *not* reacting to a child's every cry or demand. Some of the main reasons are given below:

- the more you respond to crying demands, the more your child will cry
- children need to learn to restrain their own wishes to fit in with the needs of others
- part of growing up is to learn how to become less dependent on others
- children have to learn to cope with at least some of their feelings of discomfort on their own, without letting it spread to others all the time
- it is helpful for children to be able to manage their feelings of worry and fear so that they can be comfort-

able with a reasonable level of anxiety and not need to
depend on an adult for their security
- children can only gain self-confidence by achieving
  something on their own; parents who always respond
  to their child's worries will inhibit the development of
  self-confidence
- if a child feels that it is possible to control adults by
  crying, the feeling of being small and dependent and,
  at the same time, all-powerful and omnipotent will
  eventually result in increasing insecurity and anxiety.

Coping with fears and phobias

Fears and phobias are so common in children that they
can be regarded as part of normal development. However,

FEARS HAVE TO BE FACED....

that doesn't mean that nothing needs to be done about them. An important part of growing up is the gradual gaining of confidence and the feeling that worries and fears can be mastered and controlled. The first step in the process of dealing with anxiety is to learn how to cope with separation and then being able to be alone at night. If these early steps have not been achieved, there is little point in trying to help your child cope with other fears and phobias.

Assuming that you have already dealt with the separation anxiety phase of emotional development, childhood fears and phobias should be relatively easy to sort out. The most important thing to remember is that *fears have to be faced*. The more that worries and fears are avoided, the worse they are likely to become. However, some childhood fears are very short-lived and in these cases it is obviously best not to make too much of it. If a fear or phobia has been present for a month or longer, or if it is very intrusive into everyday life, here are some ideas about what you can do to help your child.

- Be calm and confident yourself. Remember how catching anxiety can be.
- Avoid reassuring your child too much. Too much reassurance may make your child think that there really is something to worry about.
- Talking too much about your child's fears and phobias can make them worse, so be careful that you can't be overheard when you talk to other people about it.
- Carefully plan in advance how you are going to help your child to face up to the fear. There are several ways of doing this.

1.   Very slowly, in tiny graduated steps, help your child to get closer to the fear. Arrange each step to be so easy that your child is able to avoid feeling anything more than slight anxiety. If there is any sign of real fear, then you are going too fast or taking steps that are too big—in which

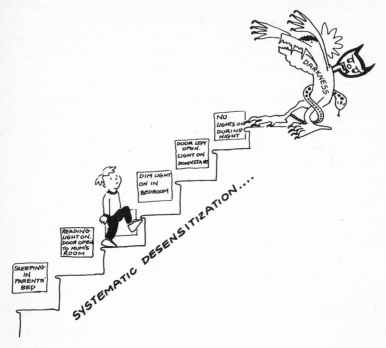

case you should go back to an earlier stage where you
know that your child could cope. This approach is called
systematic desensitization and can take a long time to
achieve anything, as well as demanding a great deal of
patience.

2.   It may be possible to show by example that there is
nothing dangerous about the feared object or situation. A
fear of insects might be dealt with by showing your child
that you don't mind insects crawling all over you! This
approach is called modelling and it may not impress your
child if the fear is very strong.

3.   A more dramatic and sometimes very effective way of
dealing with childhood fears is to expect your child to be
able to cope and carry on as if there were no problems at
all. In other words, you insist that your child has to

manage the fear, in spite of all the obvious worry and anxiety. This is a high-risk – high-gain approach. You may be able to sort things out and give your child a lot of confidence all in a very short time. On the other hand, if one of you gives up half way through, it could make things worse. This method is a bit like learning to swim in the deep end of the swimming pool—it is safe so long as there is somebody encouraging and supervising to make sure that the child doesn't give up.

4.   Another way of dealing with fears is to think about them in a positive way. There are many ways of doing this. One example would be for the child to find out everything about the feared object and possibly make a collection or a scrap-book on the subject. Another approach is to get children to relax (see page 50) and imagine themselves coping with the fear.

Whichever method you use to help your child, it is important that childhood fears may appear to be quite overpowering, but they must be more transient and variable than adult fears and easier to deal with. It is often a good idea to use several approaches in combination and never to become too serious about it.

Going to a child-minder

Many parents are unable to look after their children during the day because they have to go out to work. Therefore, a day nursery or child-minder may be necessary before a child has reached the stage of being able to cope happily with separations. Children from 3 years old should normally be able to manage being with a child-minder. The relationship with a child-minder is usually one-to-one for much of the time. It is similar to the parent–child relationship and is usually easier for children to cope with than going to a nursery. However, if your child seems anxious or distressed as a result of being with a child-minder, you should consider what is going wrong, especially if the child is able to cope with other separations quite well. Some child-minders are less competent than others and may not be able to meet the needs of all children, even if they are registered child-minders.

Separation problems are much more likely under the age of 3 years, so it can be quite a dilemma to know what to do if a child under that age has to be minded and there are no other options. If your child is obviously finding the separation difficult, then it is best to slow down the separation process. In other words, you should drastically reduce the time that your child spends away from you to the point where the distress is minimal. Once you can be confident that the child can happily cope with this short time away from you, the period of separation can gradually be extended. Sometimes, if a child is clearly very distressed by separations, it is best to stop the child-minding altogether, to give more time to work on happy separations (see page 55).

Starting at nursery

Under the age of 3 years, many children will find play groups or nurseries difficult to cope with, because the experience is so different from home. However, somewhere between 3 and 5 years it is important for all children to become confident in a peer group and at the same time to be away from home and their parents—otherwise it is easy to predict that there will be separation problems on starting at school.

Play groups and nurseries vary a great deal in how they are organized, some allowing a lot of unsupervised play and free expression, and others being more structured, with a clear programme of activities. On the whole, most children find it easier to cope with the more organized and structured settings. Predictability helps children to feel more secure and less anxious. Before finally choosing a nursery, it is helpful to visit each one so that you know exactly what is available locally and how they are organized. This is better than automatically going for the nearest or the one that your friend's children go to.

Most nurseries allow parents to stay with their children if necessary, but it can be difficult to know how best to plan this so here are some guidelines.

● It is best to keep the time that you spend at the nursery to the minimum necessary to allow your child to settle.
● For each child there is a critical time when it is best for the parent to leave. If you go too soon the child will be upset, but if you stay too long this will make your child even more upset because your presence comes to be expected.
● Most nurseries have a standard way of dealing with separation problems, so it is best to follow their advice in the first instance.
● It is helpful to have a plan worked out in advance so that you know exactly what to do.
● The time that you spend at the nursery should be

but I **don't want** to go home...
I want to stay and play **here!**

ANY INITIAL **SEPARATION PROBLEMS** SHOULD SETTLE DOWN IN A FEW DAYS....

steadily reduced—each time going a little bit earlier than your child might like, but not enough to cause great distress.

In most cases any initial separation problems should settle down in a few days and not drag on for weeks, if these guidelines are followed. However, if serious separation anxiety does occur there are several different ways of dealing with it (see Chapter 1 for background information). There are three main approaches:

1.   The 'call it a day' approach involves stopping the separations altogether, either by staying at the nursery all the time yourself or by not sending your child to the nursery at all. This is reasonable to do if you think that your child isn't really ready for separations yet or if you feel that the nursery is unsatisfactory. But remember that your child will have to be able to cope well with separation before starting school at 5 years old.

2.   The 'in at the deep end' approach is surprisingly quick, effective and successful. However, strong nerves are needed all round! This method involves handing your child over and leaving immediately. It is predictable that your child will cry, scream and be distressed, but this usually only lasts for a few minutes. Even if the distress is great at the time of separation, no harm will be done if your child is able to settle down within a few minutes. It is worth remembering that children with separation anxiety almost always settle more quickly if their parents are not present.

3.   The 'slowly slowly, bit by bit' approach is safe, but can be long and drawn out, lasting weeks or months. Each step in the separation process is mastered and consolidated before the next one is attempted. Frequently this does not progress smoothly and it isn't unusual for children to un-expectedly dig their heels in and refuse to make any progress. This is more likely to happen if progress is being

made too slowly. If your child refuses to go on to the next stage, you can either go back to an earlier stage that you know your child will be happy with or try the 'in at the deep end' approach.

Starting at school

If you have helped your child with happy separations up to the point of starting at school, there shouldn't be too many problems. However, there are a few special things that you can do with your child to make sure that everything goes smoothly:

- start talking about going to school several weeks or even months before the starting date to give it an attractive image
- make a strong link in the child's mind between growing up and going to school
- visit the school with your child before the time comes to start there—at first just point out the school as you pass by, then visit when you know the school will be empty, without children shouting and rushing around
- try to arrange an introduction to the teacher who has the class that your child will enter.

One of the reasons starting at school is such a big step in growing up is because it will probably be the first time that children are viewed in an objective way by people outside the family. Children at school have to prove themselves in a world where the adults may neither like them nor be impressed by everything that they do.

The first day that your child goes to school is a major step towards independence. It will be difficult for both you and your child to avoid very strong feelings of anxiety about the separation. The strength of the emotions takes most parents by surprise because the feelings are so powerful. At the same time the emotions are a confusing mixture of anxiety and loss together with a sense of excitement. These strong emotions can easily get in the way of normal development and cause problems—so try to keep them hidden from your child. To do this you will have to be a convincing actor or actress! Don't worry if you aren't totally successful in hiding your feelings from your child, because all parents and their children are so well attuned to picking up each other's moods that it is almost impossible to keep the feelings separate.

Most parents find that as soon as the first sign of any reluctance to go to school occurs, it is best to be very determined and as tough as is needed to get the child to school. If your child comes to believe that being at school is negotiable, it won't be long before there are major school attendance problems. It is possible to take this firm line with confidence because by 5 years old children should have reached the stage where they are mature enough to cope with separation. The only exception to this might be where a child is ill or very immature and delayed in development.

If there are problems and your child becomes distressed on the way to school, or even before leaving home, then it is important to work out what is going on—it could be one or more of the following problems.

● Separation anxiety is always at its worst at the point of separation from the parent, whether this takes place at home or at school.
● School phobia becomes stronger as the school is approached and is at its worst on arrival at school.
● Real fear is an important reason for not wanting to go to school. Is your child being picked on or bullied by other children or even by a teacher? Is your child able to cope with the work reasonably well or is it too difficult?
● Has the child a very good reason for not going to school—or is it just that, given a choice, staying at home would be preferable to going to school?

- Is it possible that your child has picked up from you that you would rather like to have company at home and wouldn't be too upset if the child stayed off school for a day or two?

If there is no satisfactory or understandable reason for not wanting to go to school, then press on with being firm about getting your child to school. If you give your child the benefit of the doubt at this early stage, you will soon find school-days even more difficult to cope with. Taking a firm line may involve getting a stubborn child dressed or even being prepared to take a half-dressed child to school. As soon as it is obvious that you are determined about going to school, all resistance usually falls away.

It may be that your child will become steadily more distressed as you get nearer to the school. The crunch time usually comes when you arrive at the school or when you have to say goodbye. This is the time to keep your nerve. Carry on as if nothing out of the ordinary is happening. The look of determination in your eyes should be all that is needed for your child to realize that there is no point in making a fuss! If your child is still not impressed with your determination, the crying, tantrums and even screaming may start. At this stage, it is best to get your child into the classroom and, as soon as you can, hand your child over to someone you can trust—give a quick explanation and then leave immediately.

Almost invariably, children settle down very soon after their parents have left, which is annoying, but is in fact a reassuring sign. This approach may seem very tough and unloving in its determination to go against the wishes of the child, but the alternative of allowing children to stay at home and dictate their demands is fraught with danger. For example:

- children will expect to have their own way on other things and will become increasingly demanding
- if a child is allowed to feel more powerful than the

parents, this usually results in feelings of insecurity and anxiety
- when children miss school for whatever reason, this is likely to cause additional problems because they get behind with the work and out of the habit of going to school
- most children are concerned to do the right thing and want to be like other children; staying off school makes them feel different, with the result that they become increasingly isolated, irritable and miserable
- avoiding the feared situation actually makes the fear worse and provides no way of finding out that the fear is manageable after all.

Once your child has settled into the routine of going to school, you are much less likely to have problems. However, if problems do occur, here are some guidelines so that you can work out what is going on.

- First of all, you should make sure that your child is not ill. It is usually obvious if your child is really ill, but if the symptoms are very non-specific such as headache, tummy ache or leg ache, it can be difficult to tell whether or not these are due to being emotionally upset.
- If you are not sure whether the symptoms are due to physical illness or to emotional upset, try the 'thermometer test'. Take the child's temperature; if it is normal, you can assume that your child is well enough to go to school. However, if you are still not satisfied with your child's condition, in spite of a normal temperature, you should seek medical advice.
- Children are sometimes sick with the tension and stress of leaving home and going to school. Once you have made sure that the child is not physically ill and has no temperature, it is best to continue going to school as usual, but to bear in mind that your child is finding either school or the separation difficult.

● If your child is finding school difficult you should investigate further and visit the place to find out what is going on. Remember the checklist:

the other children –	teasing, bullying, friendships?
the teachers –	aggressive, threatening, unsympathetic?
the school –	noisy, dirty, crowded?
the work –	too hard, or too easy?

● The cause of the problem may be at home rather than at school. Your home may be so cosy that the child does not want to go to school, or your home may be unsettled either through illness or relationship difficulties, so that when the children are at school they worry about home and want to be there to make sure that all is well.

Each of these causes has a fairly obvious solution, but don't expect it to be easy because school refusal taps into a whole wide range of complex individual and family issues. This is one of the reasons for dealing with school attendance problems in a firm and straightforward way; otherwise you could find yourself going round in circles trying to sort out what is going on. However, it is important to remember that it is only reasonable to be tough with your child about going to school if you are certain that there is no sign of illness and that there are no major problems at school.

Going to the doctor or the dentist

Everyone tends to feel anxious about seeing the dentist, and children quickly pick this up from their parents, even without a word being spoken. However, because a visit to the dentist is so much part of the everyday life it is a good idea to help your child cope well with this experience right from the start. Here are some ideas that you can try:

- arrange with the dentist that your child can go to the surgery with you just to say 'hello' and to try out the chair on several occasions
- ask if your child can watch you having your teeth examined and then have the dentist examine your child's teeth

- try to make the visit to the dentist an occasion to look forward to because of something exciting that you are going to do afterwards
- play 'going to see the dentist' games at home so that your child learns what might happen
- find out what is likely to be done to your child—what will be put in the mouth, what noises are there in the dentist's surgery, what position will the child be in the chair—and try these out at home until your child feels quite comfortable about them
- some dentists are much better with children than others: if you aren't satisfied then why not change to another who is good with children—you can find out by asking other parents.

A few children develop a phobia of dentists which makes it impossible to do anything to their teeth without resorting to all-in wrestling! If your child has developed a dental phobia, it may help to go through the guidelines above, but take it very slowly, always trying to keep the feelings of panic under your child's control. If you find yourself becoming upset as well, it may help to find someone else to be involved instead of you. As soon as you have identified a problem it is important to deal with it straight away, otherwise each panic will make the next one even worse. Should you find that your child is completely stuck with the phobia of dentists, then it may help to ask your dentist for a referral to a unit where they specialize in children with dental phobias.

Fears of going to see the doctor can be dealt with in much the same way as going to see the dentist. The problem shouldn't be so bad because generally there is no discomfort and the consultation is shorter. In both cases it is important to avoid saying 'Don't worry, the doctor/dentist won't hurt you'. This only gives children ideas about being hurt which they hadn't even thought about before!

Going into hospital

It isn't surprising that going into hospital is associated with worries and fears. We all have a fear of illness which in turn is linked with a fear of hospitals and even if your child is very young, the anxiety can easily be caught from you. Once again, this is a time when it helps to keep as much of your own fears to yourself as possible and put on an Oscar-winning performance of calmness and confidence! The anxiety that children have when they are in hospital has several components:

1. **separation anxiety—being away from parents and home**

2. stranger anxiety—being among so many unknown people
3. fear of the unknown and unfamiliar
4. 'second-hand' fear picked up from others
5. realistic fear of illness and disease.

The problems that children face on being admitted to hospital is well recognized, which is why children's wards have a policy of open visiting and parents are encouraged to stay with young children for long periods. Most wards have some facility for a few parents to stay overnight and some hospitals allow parents into the anaesthetic and recovery rooms. There is an implication that the more parents are with their child in hospital the better it is, but this is not necessarily so. The following points need to be taken into consideration.

● The need for a parent varies at different ages. Babies under the age of 6 months will have little need, provided that the standard of care is good. The need for a parent to be with a child in hospital then increases to a peak between the ages of 3 and 4 years. This is the age when hospital admission causes the most disturbance afterwards—presumably because the child is old enough to realize what is going on, but not mature enough to understand it fully or to be able to express verbally the natural worries and fears. Much older children and teenagers may benefit from not having a parent with them all the time, so that they can become involved in the life of the ward, which can be quite fun, believe it or not.
● All children have different needs for parents to be with them, depending not only on age but also on their personality, their previous experience of hospitals, and the nature of their illness.
● It is easy to forget the needs of any children at home. Sometimes it is the brothers and sisters who seem to miss out the most when a child is in hospital.

- Some parents feel so upset about their child being in hospital that they make the child more anxious rather than less.

- Although there is a lot of evidence that being in hospital causes children to be distressed, this can be expected to settle quickly in a few weeks after discharge—unless there is something else keeping the worries going.

- Because so many demands are made of parents when their child is in hospital, it is easy for them to neglect their own needs for rest and relaxation. The powerful bonds of love and affection between parent and child are at their strongest when the child is under threat. Sometimes this can lead to parents being over-involved with their child and feeling that they must do everything for the child because other people could not do it properly. It is important to realize that unless you look after yourself it will be difficult, if not impossible, to care properly for your child.

Hopefully, both you and your child will have a good relationship with the doctor who has arranged the admission to hospital. This trust and confidence will certainly help to reduce the natural worries about going into hospital, but there are several things that you can do to help your child cope with what we all know will be a stressful experience.

- Playing hospital games can be helpful, especially if they are directly relevant to what is going to happen to your child. It is possible to make or buy dolls to play the part of doctors, nurses and patients.

- Any big event like going into hospital can be coped with better if it is made as predictable as possible. It will therefore help your child if you can map out what is likely to happen and keep the visiting to a time schedule.

- Many parents find that it helps to give their child a

look... here comes the
doctor to help you feel
better....

PLAYING HOSPITAL GAMES CAN BE HELPFUL...

present to go into hospital with. The price of the
present is not as important as the comfort or distrac-
tion value.

- It is helpful to have a few familiar objects from home
  near the bed. Try to make these as visible as possible,
  rather than being tucked away in a cupboard.
- Keeping children occupied in hospital is always a
  problem. Teachers and play assistants will help, but
  you will know best what keeps your child's interest.
- It is helpful to arrange a visiting rota so that the day is
  broken up, but too many visitors can actually add to
  the stress of being in hospital.

To some extent, the issues of going into hospital are rather
like going to stay away from home for any reason, for example on a school journey or off to boarding school. Not
surprisingly, the same general principles apply for these
separations as well.

Coping with rituals and obsessions

Repeated actions and thoughts are frequently associated with worries and fears. In many ways these repetitions and rituals are anxiety-reducing and we all use these techniques for coping with daily stress—often without realizing it at all. The protective value of rituals is reduced, however, if they interfere with everyday life—for example, if a child's dressing or washing ritual results in being late for breakfast or school. Once you have decided that the ritual is unreasonable and is getting in the way of family life, then firm action needs to be taken to stop the ritual or obsession.

Preventing rituals or obsessions will usually result in a protest from children and they may try to find a way round your obstruction. Provided that stopping the ritual is done in the context of a loving family, no harm will come to the child; in fact quite the reverse. Rituals that are allowed to continue easily get out of hand and can turn into obsessions, which are more difficult to deal with because the

urge to repeat them is so much stronger.

Most rituals take up time and this can be used as a way of bringing them under control. For example, a washing ritual where everything has to be washed in a particular way, and in a certain order, may take 10 minutes to complete a task that most children would do in 2 minutes or less. In this case you could set a 2-minute time limit for the child, and if the job isn't finished it will have to be left for another time or you may have to absolutely insist that the washing is done within the time set. The use of a clock or timer alarm can be very helpful.

Taking a firm line in preventing obsessions and rituals may seem unkind, but in reality the firmness provides children with the feeling of security and comfort. The repeated actions of the ritual certainly help to reduce anxiety, but where the ritual takes over and begins to control the child, the underlying worries are only increased still further.

Try teaching your child how to relax

Young children are not really interested in relaxation—so don't expect too much! In spite of the obvious difficulty in teaching a restless and active child to be calm and restful, it is worth having a go. One advantage of teaching your child to relax is that it gives the idea that worries and tension can be brought under control and it teaches children a way of coping.

Learning how to relax is a very personal thing; there are so many different ways of relaxing that each person has to find out which is the best for them. There is always a slight risk with children that they become too self-conscious about relaxing and begin to behave like worried adults. It is therefore important to keep any relaxation practice very low-key and always good fun. Here are some suggestions of ways your child might relax:

- just being comfortable and keeping still in a quiet room
- listening to a particular piece of music that your child is fond of
- tensing up muscle groups and then relaxing them, one after the other—this method also involves breathing and thinking in a relaxed way
- tensing muscles on one side of the body and relaxing them on the other, and then alternating them.
  (These tensing methods aim to help people to gain more control over their muscles and follow the principle that if the body is relaxed then the mind will be as well.)
- repeating the same word (or mantra) over and over again
- listening to a special relaxation tape (this could be made by a parent) with instructions on being relaxed spoken in a slow and relaxing voice
- repeating short sentences about being relaxed, such as:
  'I feel relaxed'
  'I am no longer worried about . . .'
  'My whole body is floppy'
  'My mind is blank'

- thinking about a happy experience from the past
- imagining a pleasant and peaceful scene
- listening to the slow, regular tick of a large clock
- taking a deep breath in . . . and out . . . and in . . . and out.

Relaxation techniques have a mystique about them that isn't really justified. There is no right or wrong way of doing it: each person has to work out which method suits them best. If it works for your child that is good, but the same method may not work for anyone else. Do remember that too much emphasis on relaxation may actually make things worse by making it into an issue. Some people actually worry more or even panic when they try to relax!

Conclusion

Anxiety can be mastered and to some extent controlled by understanding where it comes from (how it develops) and by careful planning. It may be necessary to be very firm and confident in the way you respond to your child's worries and fears, but you should find that there is a surprisingly good response to this approach. All you need is a strong nerve!

CHAPTER 3

HOW TO DEVELOP INDEPENDENCE AND SELF-CONFIDENCE

When should you become worried about the signs of anxiety in your child? So much of any child's anxiety is normal and necessary for safety that it would be dangerous for a parent to try and stop their child from having everyday worries and fears. It should be obvious if your child is over-anxious or too worried, but if you are not sure try asking other friends and relatives what they think and listen to what your child has to say. Always take what other people say with a pinch of salt—nobody knows your child as well as you do!

Don't be surprised if you find it difficult to be objective in your assessment of your child's worries. This is because anxiety is so catching and it may not be easy to tell which are the child's anxieties and which are yours. The very close relationship between a child's and a parent's anxiety is seen when the child is worried about separation. If you observe closely you will notice that the parent often clings to the child just as much as the other way round.

Becoming independent

One of the most difficult things about being a parent is getting the right balance between dependence and independence for your child. The parent's wish for a child to be close and the wish for them to grow up are in conflict with each other. However, an inevitable part of growing up is for children to separate from the family in order to become independent. All parents have a picture in mind of how they would like their child to be in the future—a happy, self-confident person, who is making the most of life, is what most parents would want. To achieve this, the child will have to separate away from the close, protective care of the parent.

The process of becoming independent involves change, and change will always involve anxiety. In order to change, you have to leave the past behind and in doing so you lose something. It is therefore not surprising that any big change in a person's life is associated with feeling anxious and miserable, as well as excited and pleased if it is a change for the better. These mixed emotions can be very puzzling for parents as they watch their child change and develop.

The relationship between child and parent should gradually change as the child grows older, moving from the protective authority of the parent to a relationship of equals. The skill of good parenting is to get the rate of the change just right.

Another of the special skills of being a parent lies in keeping the balance between dependence and independence which, of course, changes at each stage of development. During this time the main values and goals that parents have for their children should stay the same, but the way that they are reached should change as the child grows older. At each stage a child requires a different approach.

1. A baby must have total protection and care.
2. A toddler requires considerable control and authority.
3. A young child should have supervised exposure to the outside world.
4. A school-aged child should be allowed to experience stressful events away from home in ways that are carefully planned and safe. Teenagers usually make a break for freedom and independence whatever you do!

The way in which a child is helped to separate and to deal with the anxieties of independence is crucial to how well your child will do in the long run. Here are some guidelines.

Carefully plan happy separations

Growing up and becoming more separate from a parent should happen gradually over a long period. The sooner you start the better because:

- At some time between birth and 6 to 8 months of age babies become aware of separations for the first time and will probably protest if handed to a stranger.
- If you start giving your baby short experiences of being away from you from an early age you will be able to spot exactly when the baby is reacting to separations: at this stage you will need to plan further separations very carefully.
- If your baby is used to short separations before 6 months of age and you continue with this on a regular basis, there should be less of a problem with separation later on.

It is really important to make sure that each separation you arrange is planned in such a way that you can be as certain as possible that your child will be happy during this time. Then, when your child is comfortable with a particular stage of separation, you can go on to the next step. But take it slowly; there is plenty of time if you have planned things properly.

Leave your child for progressively longer periods

Try to plan separations so that the process is a gradual one and the period of separation becomes steadily longer. It may be helpful to have a list of graded separations in your mind, such as:

1. being held by a stranger for a few minutes
2. sleeping in a separate room
3. being left with a relative or friend for a few minutes
4. being left alone in another room while you are elsewhere in the home
5. being left at home with someone who is not the parent
6. going to the home of a friend, first with the parent and then being there without the parent
7. gradually increasing the time away from the parent up to a whole day away
8. starting at play school or nursery
9. staying overnight with a friend or relative
10. beginning at primary school
11. staying away from home for a few days
12. going out to the local shops alone
13. going on public transport alone
14. starting at secondary school

Each stage in the separation process should be solidly established before going on to the next step forwards, but don't be surprised if your child slips back. Development is never a smooth process. Children typically make progress by taking two steps forwards and then one step back.

Hide your own anxiety as best you can

Although all parents have very strong feelings about their children, it is important to keep the feelings under reasonable control. This is particularly true when it comes to the anxiety that is associated with separation of a child from a parent. The combination of the strong emotions of separation and the 'infectious' nature of anxiety causes all kinds of problems for children and their parents. It is quite easy to deal with these early on, but if nothing is done the problems are likely to carry on and even have an effect much later on during adult life.

It would be unnatural for you to show no worry at all when you leave your child at school or at the nursery for the first time. But children will also be anxious about starting school and will, in addition, pick up parental concern which in turn increases their worry. Before you know where you are you may have a panicky child who is clinging like a leech to you. Here are some ways in which you can control your own anxiety and worry when your child leaves you.

- Remember that it is quite normal to have strong emotions when your child leaves you. It would be very strange if you didn't. The feelings are strongest when your child is young, but they are also felt strongly at other times, even when your child is much older, such as when the child goes on a school holiday; starts at secondary school; leaves home; gets married. Don't be surprised or worried about these normal feelings.
- If you know that you are likely to feel anxious, you will be able to recognize the feeling at an early stage before it has a chance to get out of hand. Feelings are always easier to manage and cope with when they first develop.
- The anxiety of separation will be much less if you take it in small steps, one at a time. So, when your child starts at nursery school, for example, or goes away without you, there should be a gradual build-up to this point. Then the step towards independence is not too large and the anxiety is more manageable.
- Forward planning is helpful, so that both you and your child know in advance what to expect. Go through what is likely to happen in your imagination until you feel reasonably comfortable with it, and make sure that things work out in imagination as you would like them to in reality!

- Part of your anxiety is to do with concern about what may happen to your child without your protection, but part is related to worry about how upset you might feel without your child near you. You must therefore plan carefully what you are going to do during the time your child is away from you and keep busy.

PLAN WHAT YOU ARE GOING TO DO
WHILE YOUR CHILD IS AWAY FROM YOU....

Avoid clinging to your child

Even with the best planning in the world, things can still go wrong on the day. This is because you can't control everything, particularly people outside your immediate family. If your child does become upset about leaving you, any delay in the separation will only prolong the agony. This is the time to hand the child over to someone you can trust and leave as soon as possible. Whatever you do, don't cling to your child. It is amazing how many parents find themselves clinging on to a child who is frightened to separate. However, holding on to your child will give the message that you don't want to separate and that you think it might be dangerous for the child to leave you. This is just another example of how difficult it is to be a parent and how sometimes you have to go against your natural instincts.

If you find that you have gone too fast for your child, expecting separation and self-confidence to be achieved too quickly, all you have to do is to take it more slowly from the stage that you know the child can easily cope with. Problems will only occur if you become upset and worried yourself and stop helping your child to separate and to be confident without you. If you think that all your careful planning to help your child to be confident and self-assured isn't working out, take a break, relax a while—and then start again, taking into account whatever it was that spoilt your plans last time round. Perhaps the most important thing of all about being a parent is to keep going and not give up when you don't seem to be having much success.

Shyness and friendships

Shyness is a particular form of low self-confidence and is sometimes called social anxiety. Shy children may be quite confident at home and in situations that don't involve social relationships. All children go through a phase of stranger anxiety or shyness that starts around 6 months of age and then, over the next few years, a balance has to be learnt between being too shy and being too familiar. Hopefully this will have been achieved before your child starts at school.

It takes some time to teach a child how to cope with social relationships and, even as adults, most of us are still learning about relationships and trying to get them right. You can't start too early, but don't panic if your child finds relationships difficult—just keep on working at it and doing what you can to help. The development of friendships is a very subtle process and each person has their own unique way of managing it. Parents frequently worry about their children's friendships, so here are some guidelines.

- Children vary a lot in how friendly they are, but most children need more help and guidance with their friendships than parents realize.
- It is worthwhile remembering that children will tend to copy their parents in the way they form relationships.
- In the early stages of learning about friendships (up to about 8 years old) your child will require a high level of supervision when with friends, to ensure that all goes well.
- As children grow older the supervision can be more distant, for example by being in another room or by checking what they are doing from time to time.
- Don't expect young children to be able to manage friendships well if they are unsupervised for very long. As a rough guide you can expect some form of difficulty to occur within five minutes for 5-year-olds and younger, within fifteen minutes for an 8-year-old, and within forty-five minutes at 11 years old.
- Many children have difficulty in forming relationships and it is not necessarily a sign of disturbance in the child. Some perfectly normal children prefer to be on their own.
- Be prepared to intervene if you feel that there are problems in the relationship or if friends have been chosen who are leading your child astray.

Maintaining good relationships is a delicate process that can't be forced, so be prepared to give time and space. Friendships are a bit like flowers—they need plenty of looking after in the early stages and the pests need to be

FRIENDSHIPS ARE A BIT LIKE FLOWERS....

kept away. Only later on is it safe for them to face the outside world without protection, but even then they need to be tended and cared for. Here are some ways to help your child develop good relationships.

- When you start inviting children to come and play, only have one child at a time.
- Only invite children who you think will get on well with your child.
- Don't feel bad about being selective over which friend you invite to your home.
- If you feel a particular friend is a bad influence on your child, it is quite reasonable to tell your child to keep away from them.
- When you invite a child to your home, it is a good idea to keep the visit short and happy. The longer the stay, the more likely it is that there will be tears or

arguments. As soon as the children can cope with a short time together, you can gradually increase the length of the visit.

- If the parent of the friend comes too, remember to continue to supervise and don't get distracted by interesting adult talk.

- A common problem occurs when the friend's parent has different standards of discipline and behaviour from yours. Many friendships have been lost in this way. It is therefore a good idea to sort out with the other parent who is in charge of what. A reasonable plan is to agree that you make the rules in your house and they in theirs. Whatever you agree, don't forget to tell the children!

Even the most shy and unassured child can be helped to be more confident socially if you follow the guidelines above. The important thing with shy children is to plan social contacts carefully in advance and take things very slowly with only gradual steps towards closer relationships.

How to build up your child's confidence

Self-confidence can't be developed on praise alone. It is success and achievement that build up confidence and this can only happen if your child has actually done something. In other words, confidence comes from action and activity, from having a go rather than avoiding situations and being passive. Many activities are rewarding and confidence-building in themselves, for example, learning to walk, being able to draw a recognizable picture, running quickly. However, other activities are not so obviously rewarding and it is important for parents to remember to praise these as well if they wish to give a boost to their child's self-image. Here are some examples of everyday activities that you could use as an excuse to give praise:

- getting dressed without any help
- coming to the meal table the first time asked
- helping without being asked
- remembering to clean the teeth
- putting toys away without having to be nagged
- being polite
- tidying up without being asked.

None of these activities is remarkable or out of the ordinary in any way, but each one gives an extra opportunity for you to give a boost to your child's confidence. Some children seem to be naturally confident and sail through life's problems with very little worry. Other children are natural worriers. They see the worst in everything, including themselves. They quickly lose confidence and become anxious when difficulties arise. Although some of this may be due to a lifelong personality characteristic, much of it is due to life experiences and it is this part that you can have some influence over. It is important to recognize lack of confidence in your child at an early stage, because it can become fixed as a way of life if it is just ignored. The following signs should make you consider the possibility that a child lacks self-confidence:

- avoiding doing things that might be difficult
- hesitating before doing even slightly difficult tasks
- frequently asking for reassurance
- expecting failure
- often asking for help
- thinking in a negative way and being pessimistic
- being quiet and withdrawn
- repeatedly asking questions where the answer is obvious
- acting big and being over-confident.

If three or more of these signs are present, you should suspect that your child has developed a lack of confidence and do everything you can to improve things. A lack of confidence is more likely to develop in the following circumstances:

- there are higher expectations than can be met
- the child has been excessively teased or bullied
- others in the family are obviously more successful
- the child has an over-anxious temperament
- other members of the family also lack confidence
- the child has experienced frequent failure
- the family has been unsettled
- the child has frequently experienced strong negative feelings such as anger, jealousy, misery or rejection.

Watch your child carefully if any of these conditions occur in your home because a child's confidence can be so easily undermined. The special risk for children with low self-confidence is that they will avoid activities and will therefore have little chance of making things better. However, there are many things that you can do to help and here are some ways of building up your child's confidence.

- Give extra praise for everyday activities, as outlined above.
- Set up situations where you know that your child will be able to succeed. Start with something that you know can be achieved quite easily and very gradually make the task harder, but never before the previous stage has been successfully achieved.
- Protect your child from failure.
- Avoid using negative statements about your child, such as, 'You are hopeless'; 'I have no confidence in you'; 'I knew you wouldn't be able to do it'.
- Make sure that you haven't set standards for your child that are too high.
- Show that you do have confidence in your child—and say so, too.
- Point out and emphasize every success.

- Tell your friends, in front of your child, how pleased you are with any achievement.
- Deal with any jealousy that your child may have, because this emotion is closely linked with a lack of confidence
- Make sure that no one is undermining what you are doing, especially other relatives or people at school.
- Consistent loving care and clear discipline will protect your child's self-confidence and lead to a feeling of security.

Conclusion

Growing up and becoming independent are full of excitement and fraught with danger. The rewards are big and the stakes are high, but the risks can be reduced by thoughtful planning. The aim is for children to progress gradually from a state of high supervision and external control to one of independence and internalized confidence and self-control. This is an active process and parents can't afford to be passive and hope for the best. Children normally have a powerful, unstoppable urge to grow up quickly, an urge that needs to be supervised and carefully directed.

CHAPTER 4

WORRIES AND FEARS: QUESTIONS AND ANSWERS

These questions and answers are organized in two parts. The 'Yes but. . .' section is for parents who don't really fully agree with what I have said. They have got their own ideas which are, or at least seem to be different from mine. So they put their own point of view. The 'What if. . .' section is for parents who generally agree with what I have said but can see all the problems and pitfalls.

Yes but . . .

'I think you expect parents to be much too tough with anxious children'

Unfortunately, if you are very soft and understanding with childhood anxieties, it tends to make them worse. Children look to their parents for guidance on how to cope with problems and can be helped by their parents taking a firm and confident line. Anxiety doesn't usually respond to logical reasoning—like other emotions, it is very unpredictable and is able to feed on itself and grow out of control unless you take hold of it firmly.

'Many people say that nail biting, thumb sucking, bed wetting, tics and stuttering are

signs of underlying anxiety and tension—so why haven't you mentioned them?'

Because they are not signs of anxiety. They are all habits and, like everything else, they become worse with anxiety and that is where the relationship ends. In fact, it is difficult to think of anything much that actually gets better with worry and fear. Each of these habits can also be made worse by excitement, boredom or tiredness and has a slightly different cause, but they can all occur as a normal part of development. Bed wetting, tics and stuttering have a physical or constitutional basis, related to neuro-developmental immaturity, and are all more common in boys. Nail biting and thumb sucking are habits left over from early childhood when everything is put into the mouth.

'I think you have put too much emphasis on separation anxiety'

Separation anxiety is probably the most frequent of all fears because it is based on the fear of loss—loss of a person, loss of status, loss of self-esteem and so on. Any change in a child's life will also involve loss, because the past has to be left behind and therefore 'lost' to the child. When children are able to cope well with separations and loss, you will find that they also cope well with other worries and fears.

'Why bother with all this stuff about separation? Leave children alone and they will grow up naturally on their own.'

Children vary a lot in how well they are able to cope with separations, even though this is an inevitable part of growing up. You can't expect a very young child to know what is the right speed to go. In fact children are usually keen to grow up too fast, while at the same time keeping some of their babyish habits as a comfort.

If a child is allowed to continue with a babyish habit such as thumb sucking, bed wetting or tantrums for a long time after starting at primary school, this is likely to delay growing up. If, on the other hand, a child is allowed to be too grown up and make too many decisions alone, you will probably find that he or she is getting out of control. By watching your child's behaviour you will be able to assess whether or not the stages of development are progressing normally. If you go too fast and expect too much, your child may return to babyish behaviour or go to the other extreme and become precocious and out of control. If you go too slowly towards independence and responsibility, your child will become increasingly immature with high levels of separation anxiety. None of these is a happy prospect. Your child's progress towards independence needs to be carefully guided each step of the way and not left to chance.

'I think that children need explanations about growing up'

It is always a good idea to tell children why they have to do something they may not be keen on, such as starting at school or having a baby-sitter while you go out. However, the explanation should be short and to the point. Try to

avoid getting into long discussions or arguments, because these won't help. In fact long explanations usually leave the child confused and muddled!

'I am a single parent and have to leave my daughter with a child-minder. I think this may cause problems later.'

You must select a child-minder you can have complete confidence in—and even then there may be problems if the approach of the child-minder is very different from your own. Young children like routine and thrive on predictability. If it is possible for your child-minder to keep to the same routines as at home, there are usually no major problems with settling in.

'Surely my son shouldn't be forced to separate if it is upsetting for him?'

There comes a time in every child's life when some independence from parents is necessary for healthy development. This separation is actually enforced by law when the child goes to school. Only a very few parents insist that their child should not separate from them, with the result that their child is very likely to remain dependent and immature.

Some children may not find it easy to separate and become independent, so it may be necessary to be quite firm. In fact this is usually the best thing to do. In most cases your insistence and firmness about the separation will make your child feel more confident and secure and therefore more able to cope with going to school and being independent. If your forcefulness does not have the desired effect it will almost certainly have highlighted what the underlying problem is. If not, you probably haven't been forceful enough!

'I have been told that 3 years old is too young to start at nursery'

There has been a trend to start children at nursery school at a younger and younger age, but there is no evidence that this makes them any brighter or do any better at school in the long run. The only exception to this might be if there are unusual problems within the home or if the child has developmental difficulties.

In the case of a 3-year-old, a lot will depend on the way in which the nursery is organized. If the nursery is relatively small (6-12 children) and well-structured with clear expectations of behaviour, if the children don't run wild, and if the emphasis is on play and developing relationships, then most 3-year-olds should be able to cope for two or three hours at a time, provided that they have been prepared for separations beforehand.

Some perfectly normal 3-year-olds will find leaving their parent and going to nursery school too stressful to cope with, particularly if the nursery is disorganized and noisy. If this is the case, it may be best to find another nursery, or wait for a few months before trying the nursery again when your child has matured a bit more.

Most 3-year-olds will find a separation of more than a few hours difficult to cope with and they may easily become distressed while at the nursery or possibly later on when the parents come to collect them again.

'I can't tell whether my daughter is anxious or depressed'

The symptoms of depression and anxiety are very similar, but true depression, rather than just feeling sad and miserable, doesn't show itself until about 7-8 years of age. This is because the two essential components of depression are thoughts of hopelessness and worthlessness. To feel hopeless, it is necessary to have a concept of time and to feel worthless there has to be a concept of personal identity. Neither of these aspects of development occurs much before 7 years old.

If you think that your daughter is depressed, it will be more obvious in her thoughts than in her behaviour: there would be evidence that she feels the future is bleak and that she thinks that she has little value. This may be accompanied by thoughts of self-harm. Anxiety has none of these characteristics.

'What about hypnosis?'

Hypnosis hasn't been shown to be any more effective than any other form of treatment for anxiety. Sometimes it can be helpful for adults, but hypnosis has been less well studied in children. The techniques of hypnosis are not much different from a combination of relaxation and parental instruction. It is possible for parents to have almost hypnotic powers over their children! For example, many children would be completely convinced if their parents were to say, 'The monster you thought was in your room has gone now and you can cope with the dark on your own'. Perhaps the most important reason for not using hypnosis is that it is better for children to have the feeling that they have mastered their anxiety by themselves rather than under the influence of hypnotic suggestion.

'I don't like leaving my daughter with a baby-sitter. I worry that she will become anxious and upset.'

There should be no problem at all until your daughter is about 6 months old. After that there may be problems due to separation anxiety. Don't put off your plans to go out, as long as you have left your child with a competent adult who you can trust. All that is needed is a bit of planning.

It will help if you can get your daughter used to the baby-sitter first and explain to the sitter what her daily routine is. Start with short separations first and gradually build up. Don't worry if she becomes upset when you leave, so long as she settles down quickly afterwards. Remember that you need a rest and a break, in order to continue the hard work of being a parent.

'How do I know how quickly my son should become independent?'

All children need to go at their own pace, but there are important goals to aim for, such as starting school or spending a night away from home. The sooner you start the preparation for separation and independence the better—then you won't have to rush things at the last minute. Your child's behaviour will tell you whether you are going at the right speed.

'At what age should I allow my daughter to go alone on public transport?'

To some extent this will depend on how safe you feel the local transport services are, but it is reasonable to aim for your daughter to be able to travel alone for short distances before she starts at secondary school. As with all steps towards independence, it is easier to go in stages and you could build up travelling skills in the following way:

1. Get your daughter to ask for the fare with you sitting beside her.
2. Travel together, but sit in different parts of the bus.
3. Go on ahead to the next bus stop and get your daughter to travel on her own to meet up with you there.
4. Put your daughter on the bus and get her to make her own way home.

5. Finally, your daughter should now be ready to go off on the bus on her own and to make her own way back home.

If at any time your child starts to find the travelling difficult, you just have to go back to an earlier stage and take it more slowly.

'My son is mentally handicapped—shouldn't I treat him differently?'

There is no reason why intellectually handicapped children should be treated any differently from other children in relation to worries and fears. The main thing to remember is that their development is much slower than normal, so the process of separation will also be slower. One way of deciding what your child should be doing is to work out roughly what developmental age he has reached and then expect him to be independent at that level.

If, for example, your son is 10 years old, but has only reached the 3-year-old stage in his development, don't be surprised if there are some problems with separation similar to those of a toddler. All you need to do is to deal with them as you normally would in a child of that age.

'Why don't you recommend the use of drugs for anxiety?'

Anxiety is so much part of normal life that it would be easy for drugs to become part of it, too. Unfortunately this happens sometimes. Very rarely, anxiety becomes so overwhelming that medication may have a part to play, but it should only be prescribed by a doctor with specialized knowledge of childhood worries and fears. Childhood anxiety is much less fixed than in adults and it generally responds very well to clear and confident management along the lines that I have indicated in this book.

What if . . .

'I can't hide how upset I am when my child leaves me'

All parents can expect to become upset when they leave their child. However, it is important to hide how you feel as much as possible. Practice is what is needed—you may need to organize a lot of short separations so that you can get your practice in!

'My daughter cries when I collect her from the nursery'

This does not necessarily mean that the separation has been too stressful for your daughter. It may be due to disappointment at having to end a good game or relief at seeing you again. If the nursery staff report no problems while you are away and your daughter is unable to explain what the reason is for crying, then it is unlikely that there is anything too seriously wrong. In this case it is best to take little notice of the crying. Just give your child a hanky and tell her to dry her eyes, blow her nose and get ready for going home.

'My son is afraid of the dark'

Most children go through a phase of worrying about the dark, most commonly between the ages of 4 and 6 years. How you respond to this will determine how well your child is able to cope, not only with the dark, but also with being alone. It is easy to respond to fear of the dark by providing light and keeping doors open. The trouble with this approach is that it gives a child the message 'the dark is dangerous'. Your son will find it difficult if not impossible to become confident in the dark unless he experiences it and it is clearly best for this to happen in the safety and security of your home.

Being alone in the dark is one of the few occasions when young children can safely gain a feeling of inner security and of being comfortable with themselves, without being dependent on outside support. The development of this inner strength and confidence is essential for children if they are to cope well with the rough and tumble of life in the outside world.

'My son has nightmares'

Dreaming is a normal part of sleeping, so don't be surprised if your child has nightmares occasionally. Like many other regular activities, sleeping and waking quickly become habits. For example, we often wake just before the alarm goes off. It is therefore helpful to get your child into a good sleep habit, with a regular time for going to bed and getting up. When you say good night, try and always use the same words, such as, 'Good night, sleep well, God bless'. These words will then become a cue for going off to sleep.

If your child regularly wakes with a nightmare, it is best to avoid going to him if you can. Should you go in, there is a risk that this will soon become part of his sleeping/waking habit and he will always wake in the night expecting you to come to him. Of course, it is sometimes necessary to go and calm children if they are very distressed by a nightmare, so here are some guidelines:

- keep what you do and say to a minimum
- stay for as short a time as possible
- tuck your child up and say your regular good night words, then leave the room
- teach your child that it is possible to take control of nightmares and either make yourself wake up or to make them have happy endings—children are better

TEACH YOUR CHILD THAT IT IS POSSIBLE TO **TAKE CONTROL**
OF NIGHTMARES AND TO MAKE THEM HAVE **HAPPY ENDINGS....**

at doing this than adults and although it sounds improbable, it can be done!

Night terrors and sleep-walking can be dealt with much the same way, but it is important not to try to wake a child in these states because they occur in deep sleep. A recent and rather experimental technique for dealing with frequently repeated night terrors suggests that you should keep a diary of the terrors to determine when they usually occur. Then all you have to do is to wake the child just before you think a terror is going to start. After a week the night terrors have usually stopped.

'I find my child's behaviour more difficult after we have been apart'

We all find change difficult and stressful, and children are no exception. As a rough guide you might expect your child to take half as long as the separation to settle back into the routine at home. If the separation was stressful it will take much longer to get back to normal.

'The nursery want me to stay with my son, but I think it is best that I leave immediately we arrive'

Nurseries and schools have different ideas on how to manage the separation of children from their parents. Staying with a child for some time or leaving immediately can both work effectively, so it is usually best to be guided by the staff of the nursery, especially if they seem to be confident about what they are doing. If there is any doubt about what you should do, it is best to leave as soon as possible. Not only is your son more likely to settle down quickly, but the amount of distress for everyone is less prolonged.

'My daughter clings to me so tightly that I can't get away'

This is a common problem and you will have to be very firm and determined. Find another adult to help you and hand the child over as soon as possible. Then leave immediately. Whatever you do, don't get cross: it will only make things worse. Just talk to your daughter as if what you are doing is completely normal and you haven't noticed that she is clinging to you.

It often helps if you tell your child what you plan to do together when you meet again, so that she has something to look forward to. Alternatively it may help for her to have something familiar to look after while you are away, such as a doll, or something belonging to you, like a bag.

'My son is afraid of dogs'

Fear of dogs is very reasonable. All dogs can be dangerous if not handled correctly, but young children often have no fear of dogs and only learn to fear them if they pick it up from someone else or if they have been hurt by a dog. The sudden reactions of a frightened child are likely to excite a dog or worry it. In either case it is important to teach children to have a healthy respect for any dog, especially if it is unknown. Here are some ways of teaching your son how to cope with dogs:

- assume that all dogs are unfriendly until proved otherwise
- when you meet a dog off the lead, walk on and take as little notice of the dog as possible
- never make any sudden movements near a dog
- never touch or even speak to a dog unless you have been introduced to it by the owner
- once the dog has been introduced, allow the dog to make friends with you and have a sniff first, before you do anything
- when you are near any dog it is best to keep your fingers out of the way unless you know it very well. It helps to teach children to keep their hand in a fist so that not only are the fingers out of the way, but by keeping a clenched fist it is more difficult for a dog to bite it and easier to get the hand out of a dog's mouth in the unlikely event of it actually biting. Although making a fist may not make that much difference to a dog, it is likely to help your child to feel more in control.

'I think my daughter may be agoraphobic'

Agoraphobia is an adult condition of neurotic anxiety that has been allowed to get right out of control. It is rare in older teenagers and never occurs before puberty. Occasionally it is possible for younger children to appear agoraphobic either because it has been picked up 'second-hand' from a parent or because it is confused with some other reason for staying at home, such as social anxiety. If childhood fears and phobias are allowed to continue and take a hold, then occasionally they will continue into adult life as agoraphobia.

'My son gets into a panic about exams'

It would of course be abnormal not to get stressed up by exams. In fact, there is good evidence that people do better if they are rather anxious—but not too much. Getting the right balance needs practice and that is what your son should do. Although it is helpful to discuss this with the school, a lot can be done at home along the following lines:

- set up little tests that last only a few minutes
- make sure that the practice tests are easy enough to succeed in
- when your son feels confident, make the tests a bit more difficult
- try to get the school to ease up on tests for a while, because it is important that your son avoids failure while he is regaining his confidence
- it may help to get your son to practise relaxation and at the same time to imagine himself in an exam at school and coping well
- gradually make the little tests more stressful, with a greater element of competition and more at stake. You will soon know if you are taking it too quickly, because it won't work, so just go a bit slower, but keep at it until as long as is necessary.

'My daughter has school phobia'

School attendance problems are dealt with in Chapter 2.

However, school phobia is a rather specific state and often confused with other conditions such as:

- separation anxiety
- realistic fear due to teasing or bullying
- concern about illness or distress in other family members at home
- feelings of depression
- playing truant (the child is neither at home or at school)
- malingering.

Children with school phobia are quite all right so long as they don't have to go to school. Usually they are bright children who cause no problems at school in behaviour or achievement. School phobic children almost always come from stable home backgrounds where there are no obvious family problems—apart from a tendency for parents to be over-involved and over-anxious. Typically, school phobia becomes worse, the nearer the child is to school, but usually settles down once in school.

On the whole, it is best to get the school phobic child back to school as quickly as possible, using whatever method seems to work even if this means being quite tough. This approach may cause a great deal of distress, but it is by far the most effective and rapid, and so prevents secondary problems arising through being out of school and getting behind with the work. If you have any doubts about this, it would help to have some professional advice.

'I have done everything you have suggested, but my child still gets very anxious and seems to have lots of worries and fears. I think I need professional help for my child.'

It is always difficult to know when is the right time to get professional help with a family problem, and even more difficult to know where to go and whom to ask. Here are some suggestions if you feel it is necessary to get some outside help.

● Ask other parents and professionals what they know of the local services, but take what they say with a pinch of salt because individual opinions may be unreliable. One of the best-informed people is likely to be your GP.
● Voluntary groups for parents can be very supportive and give you an idea of how other people have coped. They don't give professional advice, but they should be able to advise on how to get this type of help.
● There is a wide range of professional groups who have specialized training and experience with children's emotional and behavioural problems. The difference between the various professions is confusing to say the least. One way round this problem is to ask your GP to refer you to the local Child Psychiatry Service, where it is usual for a range of different professions to work closely together.
● Don't be put off a referral to a Consultant Child Psychiatrist; they are medically qualified doctors with a very broad training in the full range of children's problems. They have special skills in helping any problem of emotions or behaviour which seems to be getting out of control and out of proportion to what might be expected, given the circumstances.

APPENDIX

WHAT THE RESEARCH SHOWS

Fear and the anticipation of fear—that is, anxiety—has been studied in great detail, starting in recent times with the work of Charles Darwin who in 1872 considered the links between animal and human fear. At the turn of the century Sigmund Freud was developing the theory that anxiety was at the root of all emotional problems. Since that time considerable advances have been made in the understanding of the nature of anxiety, especially over the last few years.

Animal studies

Study of the animal kingdom has provided amazing insights into the nature of fear. For example, the way in which baby chicks show fear of a moving object can be altered by the way light is shone on the eggs before they are hatched (Salzen, 1979). If pregnant rats are handled frequently, it has been shown that their offspring show fewer signs of fear and emotional reactions (Papousek, 1979). These are just two of several studies that suggest that pre-natal experience can affect the expression of emotions after birth.

Many of the animal studies which have been carried out with rhesus monkeys have been reviewed by Stephen Suomi (1986). The monkeys show clear developmental stages of fear responses as they grow older—moving from relatively undifferentiated clinging to more complex repetitive, ritualistic behaviour. When faced with danger, the fully grown monkeys regressed to immature comfort-seeking and stereotypic movements. The physiological responses to fear appear to be much the same whatever the age, even though the behaviour is different. Young monkeys separated from their mothers show an increase in anxiety responses to further separations which can be modified by how early or frequent the separations were and other factors such as the quality of parenting and the stability of the social group.

Work with dogs has shown that there is an initial approach phase followed by a fear response to strangers that becomes obvious around the age of 5 weeks. However, this fear of strangers could be greatly reduced by daily handling (Gurski et al., 1980). There is some evidence from work with several different species that there is a critical period for bonding that occurs soon after birth. If this period is missed, then stranger anxiety and fear responses generally are increasingly difficult to modify. Other interesting findings are that animals show less evidence of fear if they are able to influence their environment and show better emotional control if subjected to controlled episodes of stress while still young (Marks, 1987).

Surveys

Worries and fears are very common in normal children. An early and now classic study by MacFarlane et al. (1954) revealed that as many as 90 per cent of children between the ages of 2 and 4 years were reported by their mothers to have one or more fears, with a peak incidence at 3-4 years. Fears of animals peaked between 2 and 4 years, and fears of the dark and of monsters peaked at 4-6 years. In their well-known study of anxiety in 4-year-olds, the Newsons (1968) found that mothers reported that approximately 70 per cent experienced fears, and it may be even higher than this because it has been shown that parents tend to under-estimate fears in their children (Lapouse & Monk, 1959). The same study found that there was no obvious relationship between the type of worries that parents had and the fears of their children.

In spite of the high incidence of worries and fears in normal children, the frequency of anxiety occurring as a problem is much lower. Richman et al. (1975) reported that 2.5 per cent of 3-year-olds experience worries that were serious enough to be seen as a problem and in 5-year-olds the rate was about 5 per cent (Golding & Rush, 1986). The incidence of worries and fears seems to be fairly equal in boys and girls until around the onset of puberty, when there is a relative decrease of reported anxiety in boys (MacFarlane et al., 1954).

Stranger anxiety

It is now well established that babies around 4 months old begin to discriminate between who they will and will not smile at. The development of stranger anxiety has been well reviewed by Professor Isaac Marks (1987). He concluded that by 4-9 months old, children show obvious fear responses to strangers (gaze avoidance, increased heart rate and crying) and these findings hold true for children from many different cultures. Stranger anxiety can be modified by a number of factors, the more important of which are outlined below:

- the setting—anxiety is more frequent if the child is on unfamiliar territory without the parent being present
- the stranger—more fear is aroused if the stranger approaches or touches the child rather than the other way round and if the approach is sudden and unexpected, and where the stranger is not responsive to the child's needs
- the child—children who have had only limited exper-

ience of people other than their parents not surprisingly show more evidence of stranger anxiety, especially if the child feels unable to influence the stranger.

There is a large variation between children in the way in which they show stranger fear. In some children the response is mild and quickly over; in others a strong reaction may persist. Bronson (1972) observed that these differences depended to some extent on the child's temperament but also on the age. Crying was a frequent reaction before 6 months, but much less frequent by 9 months. However, the strength of the stranger anxiety generally increases over the first 1-2 years including wariness to peers and in some children it carries on into later childhood as shyness (Campbell, 1986).

Separation anxiety

Separation anxiety is a universal phenomenon closely related to fear of strangers. It occurs at about the same stage of development as stranger anxiety. A review of the relevent research by Susan Campbell (1986) identified the following factors that have an effect on the intensity and duration of distress after separating a child from the parents:

- the age of the child—distress shows itself at 6-9 months and slowly reduces after 30 months
- the quality of the parent–child relationship—there is less distress if the relationship is secure and the mother is responsive and accessible to the child
- the setting—more anxiety is seen when the child is in an unfamiliar environment, such as in hospital
- previous experience—children who have had good experiences of brief, happy separations generally seem to cope well.

John Bowlby (1973) is well recognized as an authority on the effects of separation on children. He noted that if a parent–child separation is prolonged, a sequence of distressed behaviour occurs:

1. protest—crying and struggling
2. detachment—withdrawn and apparently unmoved by the separation
3. despair—appearing miserable, depressed and uninterested.

The whole field of separation has been reassessed by Professor Michael Rutter (1981). It seems that the detachment and despair phases are not invariable and are more likely to occur if there has been no preparation for the separation and if the subsequent care is unsatisfactory. Admission to hospital is less stressful for children who have previously had a good experience of happy separations and where the parent has been prepared for what is involved. Distress can also be reduced by taking in the child's toys and keeping to familiar routines. When young children are reunited with their parents they frequently show signs of anger by being openly aggressive or by avoiding them. This is more marked if the separation has been a long or stressful one (Main and Weston, 1982).

The physiology and biology of anxiety

Twin studies indicate that there is a genetic component for the more severe anxiety states associated with panic. However, adult type panic doesn't occur before 12 years of age, so it is more likely that the increased risk of anxiety states in the children of adults with agoraphobia and other panic disorders is due to environmental influences within the home. There is also some evidence that the temperamental trait that is usually described as sensitive, emotional or highly strung is also under genetic influence (Barlow, 1988).

Most of the research into the psyiology of anxiety has been carried out in adults, but there is no evidence to suggest that results would be very different in children. Regular differences have been found between anxious and non-anxious people as shown below (Lader, 1980; Barlow, 1988).

- The level of arousal is more consistently raised in over-anxious people, and increased rates and irregular fluctuations are found for the following:

  pulse rate
  blood pressure
  blood flow
  some brain functions
  muscle tension
  bowel activity
  skin sweating
  rate of breathing.

- Anxious people take longer to adjust to stress. Their levels of arousal remain high for longer than normal.
- Recent work has shown that blood flow to parts of the brain is reduced during states of panic.
- Increased output of corticosteroids from the adrenal gland occurs as a result of activity in the pituitary gland producing cortisol, but this is a non-specific response to stress and there is little difference between anxious and normal people.
- There are a number of speculative changes that involve brain receptors and a sensitivity to carbon dioxide levels.

Investigation of the physiological responses to separation in monkeys have revealed that cortisol soon returns to normal levels following reunion, but heart rate and rhythm, together with altered brain activity, remain altered for weeks afterwards (Marks, 1987). This latter finding suggests that childhood separations may have long-term adverse effects.

What happens to anxious children

Many childhood worries and fears appear to be normal and short-lived developmental phases, but follow-up studies suggest that a significant proportion of anxious children continue to experience emotional difficulties. A five-year follow up of children from the outer London borough of Walthamstow found that there was a significant association between anxiety in 3-year-olds and emotional disorders at the age of 8 (Richman et al., 1982). The world-famous study of children on the Isle of Wight, carried out by Professor Michael Rutter and his colleagues, reported that 11-year-old children with emotional problems were twice as likely to have similar problems as teenagers (Rutter, 1980). These findings supported the earlier reports that fears and shyness tend to be relatively stable over time (MacFarlane et al., 1954).

Follow-up studies of school phobic children show that the emotional symptoms have a strong tendency to continue into adult life, although it is unclear how much actual disability this causes (Gittelman, 1986). There is also evidence that over-anxious adults frequently report having been anxious as children. Ian Berg and his colleagues found that more than 20 per cent of agoraphobic women had experienced school phobia as children (Berg et al., 1974). A research review of the links between childhood anxiety and adult emotional disorders by Professor Tony Cox (1976) concluded that emotionally disturbed children have twice the risk of developing a similar problem in adult life when compared with the general population, but more reassuringly, the majority of children with worries and fears grow up into relatively normal adults.

Conclusion

The research on worries and fears has shown how frequently children experience anxieties and how these change at different developmental stages. Although emotions are a function of the mind, there is considerable evidence that they have an important physical component. The majority of children with fears and phobias seem to do well, but the long-term outlook for children with more severe anxiety disorder is less optimistic.

REFERENCES

Barlow, D. H., *Anxiety and its Disorders: The Nature and Treatment of Anxiety and Panic*, The Guilford Press (1988)

Berg, I., Marks, I., McGuire, R. and Lipsedge, M., School phobia and agoraphobia, *Psychological Medicine*, 4,428-434 (1974)

Bowlby, J., *Attachment and Loss, Vol.2 Separation*, Basic Books, New York (1973)

Bronson, G. W., Infants' reactions to unfamiliar persons and novel objects, *Monographs of the society for research in child development*, 37, (3-Serial No 148) (1972)

Campbell, S. B., Developmental issues in childhood anxiety, *Anxiety Disorders of Childhood*, R. Gittelman, (Ed), John Wiley (1986)

Cox, A., The association between emotional disorders in childhood and neurosis in adult life, *Research in Neurosis*, H. M. Van Praag, (Ed), Bohn, Scheltems and Holkema (1976)

Gittelman, R., Childhood anxiety disorders: correlates and outcome, *Anxiety Disorders of Childhood*, R. Gittelman, (Ed), John Wiley (1986)

Golding, J., Rush, D., Temper tantrums and other behaviour problems, *From Birth to Five*, N. R. Butler & J Golding (Eds), Pergamon Press (1986)

Gurski, J. C., Davis, K. and Scott, J. P., Interaction of separation discomfort with contact comfort and discomfort in dogs, *Develop. Psychobiol.*, 13, 463-467 (1980)

Lader, M. H., Psychophysiological studies in anxiety,

Handbook of Studies in Anxiety, G. D. Burrows and D. Davies (Eds), Elsevier/North Holland (1980)

Lapouse, R. and Monk, M. A., Fears and worries in a representative sample of children, *Amer. J. Othopsychiat.* 29, 803-818 (1959)

MacFarlane, J. W., Allen, L. and Honzik, M. P., *Behaviour Problems of Normal Children Between 21 Months and 14 Years*, University of California Press (1954)

Main, M. and Weston, D. R., Avoidance of the attachment figure in infancy, *The Place of Attachment in Human behaviour*, C. M. Parkes and J. Stevenson-Hinde (Eds), Tavistock (1982)

Marks, I., The development of normal fear: a review, *J. Child Psychol. Psychiat.*, 28, 667-697 (1987)

Newson, J. and Newson, E., *Four Years Old in an Urban Community*, Allen and Unwin (1968)

Papousek, H., and Papousek, M., Early ontogeny of human social interactions: its biological roots and social dimensions, *Human ethology*, M. Von Cranach, (Ed), Cambridge University Press (1979)

Richman, N., Stevenson, J., Graham, P., *Preschool to School: A Behavioural Study*, Academic Press (1982)

Richman, N., Stevenson, J. and Graham, P., Prevalence of behaviour problems in 3 year old children: an epidemiological study in a London Borough, *J. Child Psychol. Psychiat.*, 16, 277-287 (1975)

Rutter, M., *Changing Youth in a Changing Society*, Harvard University Press (1980)

Rutter, M., *Maternal Deprivation reassessed*, Penguin, (1981)

Salzen, E. A., The ontogeny of fear in animals, *Fear in Animals and Man*, W. Slukin, (Ed), Von Nostrand Reinhold, London, (1979)

Suomi, S. J., Anxiety-like disorders in young nonhuman primates, *Anxiety Disorders of Childhood*, R. Gittelman, (Ed), John Wiley (1986)

FURTHER READING

Gittelman, Rachel (Ed), *Anxiety disorders of childhood.*
John Wiley (1986)
An American textbook written by world-renowned experts—comprehensive, but rather technical.

Barlow, David, *Anxiety and its disorders: The Nature and Treatment of Anxiety and Panic.* The Guilford Press (1988)
An excellent, wide-ranging review of anxiety both normal and abnormal—very detailed, with much food for thought.

Marks, Isaac, 'The development of normal fear: a review', *J. Child Psychol. Psychiat.* Vol.28, No.5, pp.667-697 (1987)
A superb review, drawing together ethological, behavioural and physiological research.

Hersov, Lionel and Berg, Ian (Eds), *Out of School: Modern Perspectives in Truancy and School Refusal.* John Wiley (1980)
A useful book if you wany to know more about nonattendance at school and overdependency.

INDEX